Skyscrapers

Julie Haydon

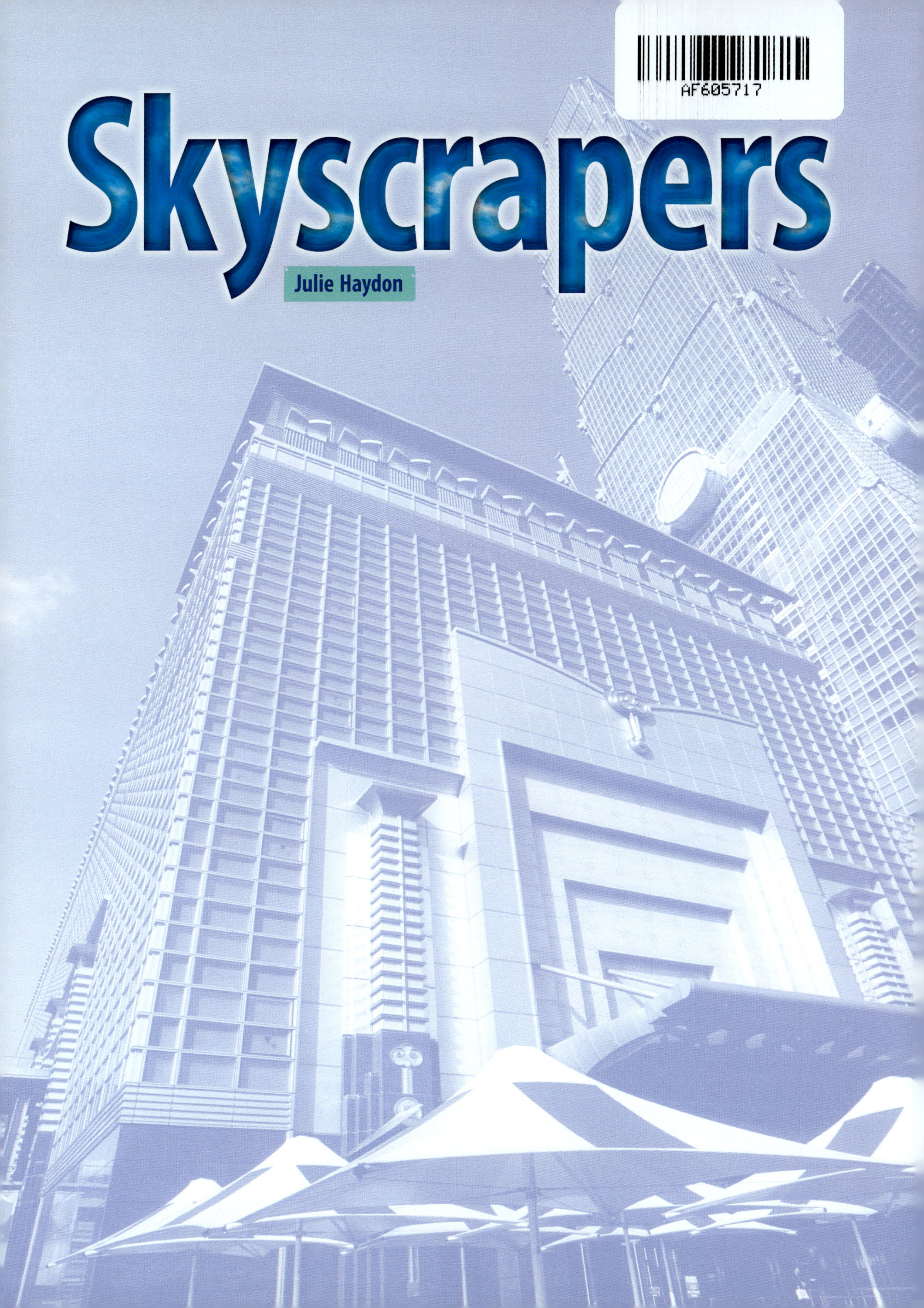

Skyscrapers

Text: Julie Haydon
Editor: Rochelle Ransom
Design: Jennifer Warwick
Series design: James Lowe
Photo researcher: Corrina Tauschke
Production controller: Adam Bextream
Reprint: Siew Han Ong

Acknowledgements
The author and publisher would like to acknowledge permission to reproduce material from the following sources:
Alamy/Dennis Cox: p. 20; Corbis/Alan Schein Photography: pp. 5 (main), back cover; Corbis/B.S.P.I.: p. 14; Corbis/Jose Fuste Raga: pp. 15, 21; Corbis/Klaus Hackenberg/zefa: p. 10 (main); Corbis/Michele Falzone/JAI: p. 19; Corbis/Patrick Robert/Sygma: p. 11; Getty Images: pp. 8, 9, 16; Impact Ltd./ www.burjdubaiskyscraper.com/Daniel Hoffmann: p. 23 (right); Jennifer Warwick © Cengage Learning Australia: pp. 7, 23 (left); Photolibrary/Austrophoto: p. 10 (inset); Photolibrary/Birger Lallo: p. 22 (left); Photolibrary/Edmund Sumner: p. 4; Photolibrary/Jeff Greenberg: pp.3, 6; Photolibrary/Johnny Stockshooter: p. 5 (inset); Photolibrary/Michele Falzone: p. 18; Photolibrary/Sylvain Grandadam: pp. 1, 17, cover; The Skyscraper Museum: pp. 12-13.

Every effort has been made to trace and acknowledge copyright. However, if any infringement has occurred, the publishers tender their apologies and invite the copyright holders to contact them.

Fast Forward Independent Texts
Level 25

For product information and technology assistance,
in Australia call 1300 790 853;
in New Zealand call 0508 635 766

For permission to use material from this text or product,
please email **aust.permissions@cengage.com**

ISBN 978 0 17 017958 4
ISBN 978 0 17 017899 0 (set)

Cengage Learning Australia
Level 7, 80 Dorcas Street
South Melbourne, Victoria Australia 3205

Cengage Learning New Zealand
Unit 4B Rosedale Office Park
331 Rosedale Road, Albany, North Shore NZ 0632

For learning solutions, visit **cengage.com.au**

Printed in Australia by Ligare Pty Ltd
3 4 5 6 23 22 21

Skyscrapers

Julie Haydon

Contents

CHAPTER 1

Skyscrapers

Skyscrapers are very tall buildings with many levels, or floors. Early skyscrapers were about 10 to 20 levels high, but modern skyscrapers often have more than 50 levels.

Skyscrapers are built in cities all around the world. Modern skyscrapers are places for people to work, live and visit for recreation.

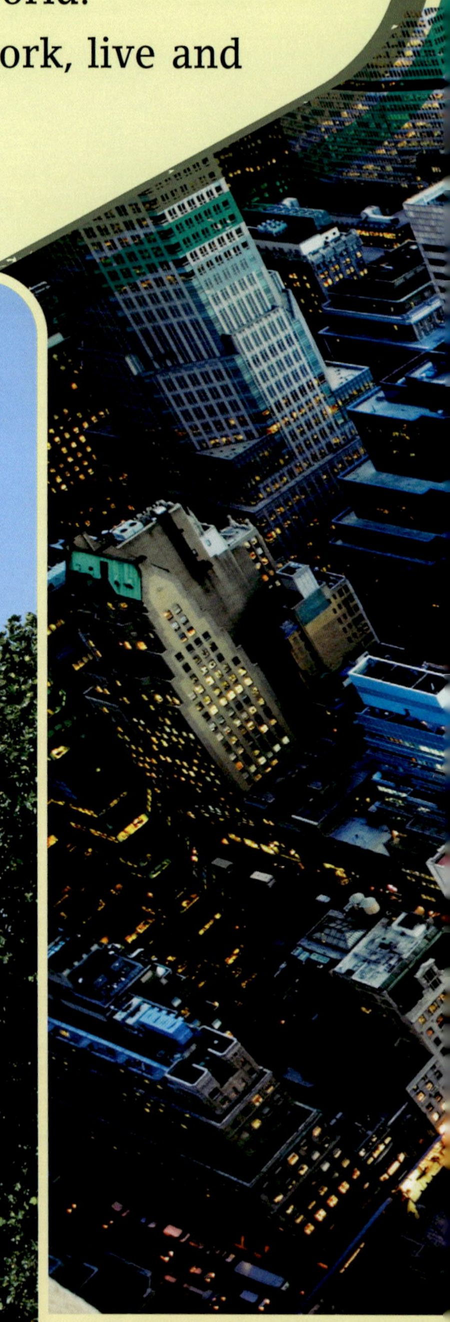

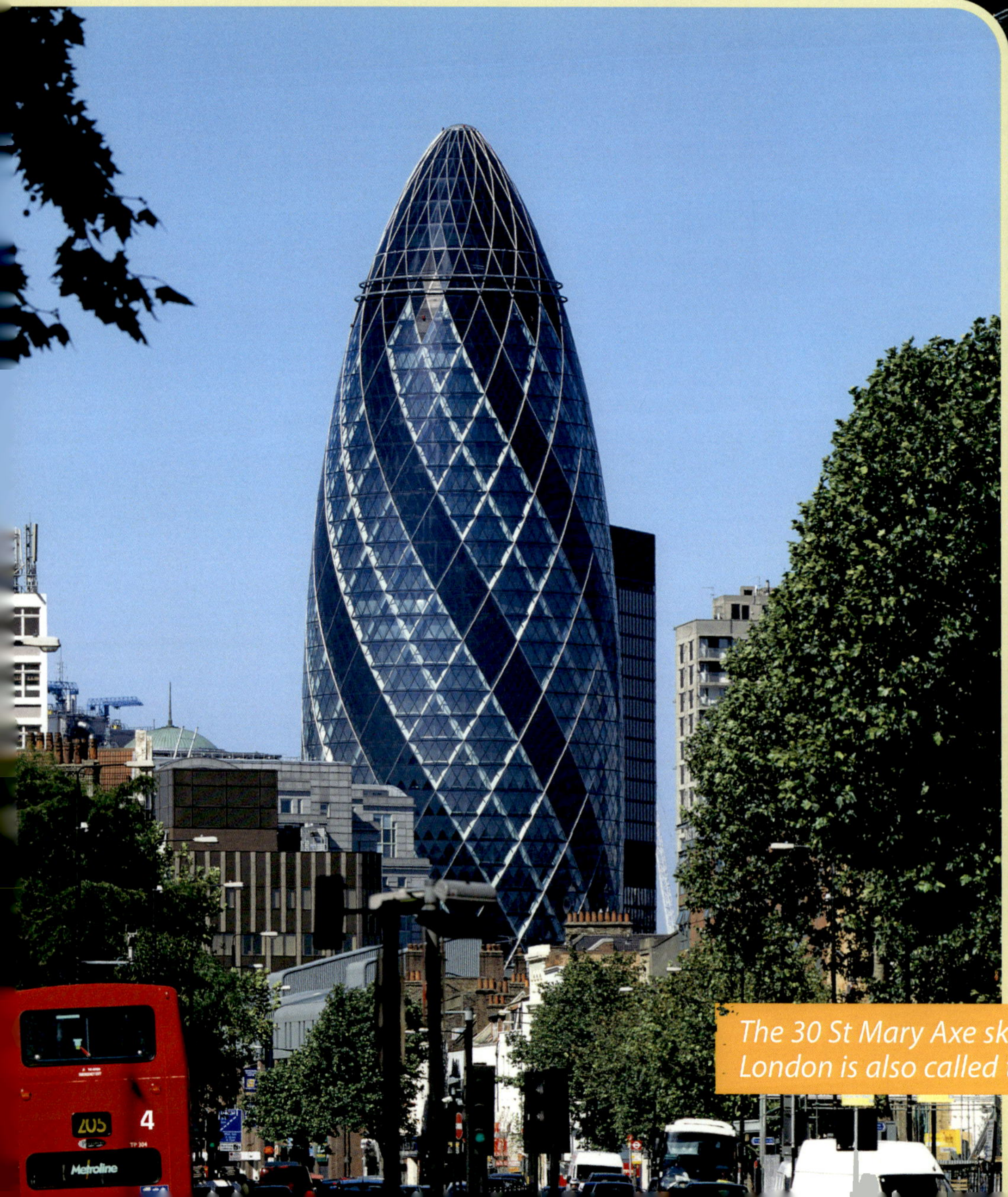

The 30 St Mary Axe skyscraper in London is also called the "Gherkin".

Skyscrapers are much taller than they are wide, but not all very tall buildings are skyscrapers. To be called a skyscraper, a very tall building must have many levels where people can have their businesses or homes.

The CN Tower in Toronto, Canada, is a tower, not a skyscraper.

Around the world, skyscrapers contain offices, apartments, shops, hotels, restaurants, cafes, museums and theatres. Many skyscrapers are major tourist attractions.

The first skyscrapers were built in the USA in the late 1800s. As cities grew, more space was needed, but land to build on became harder to find.

There is more space inside a very tall building than in a low, wide building. People learned how to safely build very tall buildings.

the Flatiron Building, New York City

They also learned how to build and safely operate lifts inside buildings. People were then able to begin building skyscrapers in cities.

As more skyscrapers were built, more people were able to come to cities to live and work. Over time, the look of some cities changed as more skyscrapers were built.

CHAPTER 2

Parts of a Skyscraper

Most skyscrapers have

- strong concrete and steel **supports** underground
- a frame made of steel, or concrete and steel
- strong walls
- glass windows
- open space around the base of the building
- lifts inside the building to move people from floor to floor.

Lifts

Skyscrapers often have a number of lifts. Passenger lifts move people from floor to floor, including the car parking levels, which are often underground.

Service lifts are used to move goods from floor to floor. Some lifts are so fast that they can travel at more than 1000 metres a minute.

Safety First

Modern skyscrapers are designed to be safe. They have the following safety features:

- stairs for people to use if there is a fire
- water tanks, so there is water on hand in case of a fire
- machines that suck smoke out of the building during a fire
- safe areas outside the building for people to go to in an emergency.

An emergency staircase is used in case of a fire.

an emergency exit sign

Skyscrapers are also designed to **withstand** wild weather, such as strong winds.

Skyscrapers that are built in areas where earthquakes occur are designed to remain standing if an **earthquake** hits.

Even so, people who live and work in skyscrapers must practise what to do in an emergency. They need to learn how to get out of the building quickly and safely.

This skyscraper remains standing after an earthquake in Kobe, Japan, in 1995.

The World's Tallest Skyscrapers (1890–2010)

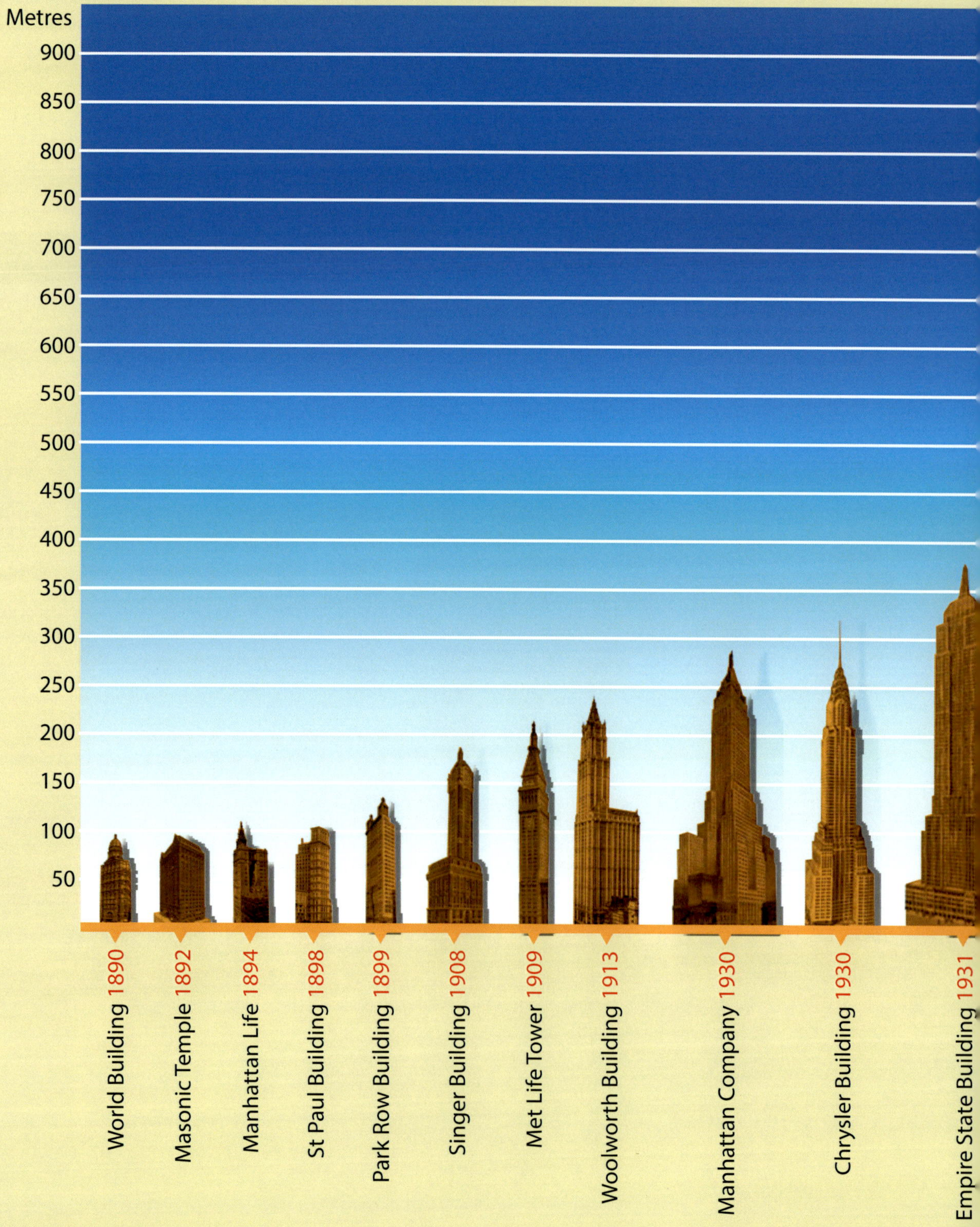

Metres
900
850
800
750
700
650
600
550
500
450
400
350
300
250
200
150
100
50

World Building 1890
Masonic Temple 1892
Manhattan Life 1894
St Paul Building 1898
Park Row Building 1899
Singer Building 1908
Met Life Tower 1909
Woolworth Building 1913
Manhattan Company 1930
Chrysler Building 1930
Empire State Building 1931

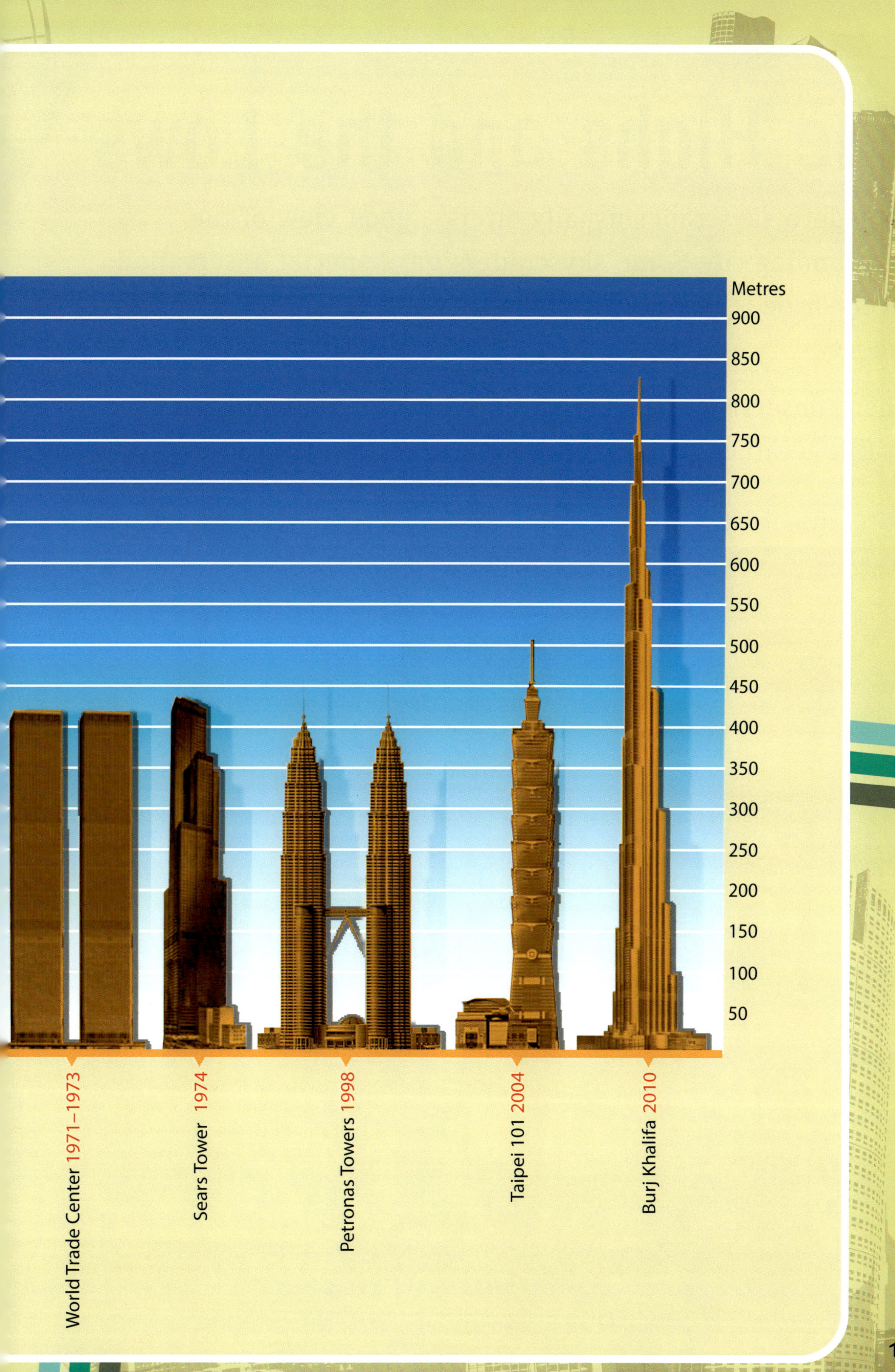
Metres
900
850
800
750
700
650
600
550
500
450
400
350
300
250
200
150
100
50
World Trade Center 1971–1973
Sears Tower 1974
Petronas Towers 1998
Taipei 101 2004
Burj Khalifa 2010

CHAPTER 4

The Highs and the Lows

A modern skyscraper usually offers a good view of the surrounding city. Some skyscrapers have special observation levels or decks where people can go and look out safely over the city.

These observation levels are often popular tourist attractions. In fine weather, people can see great distances.

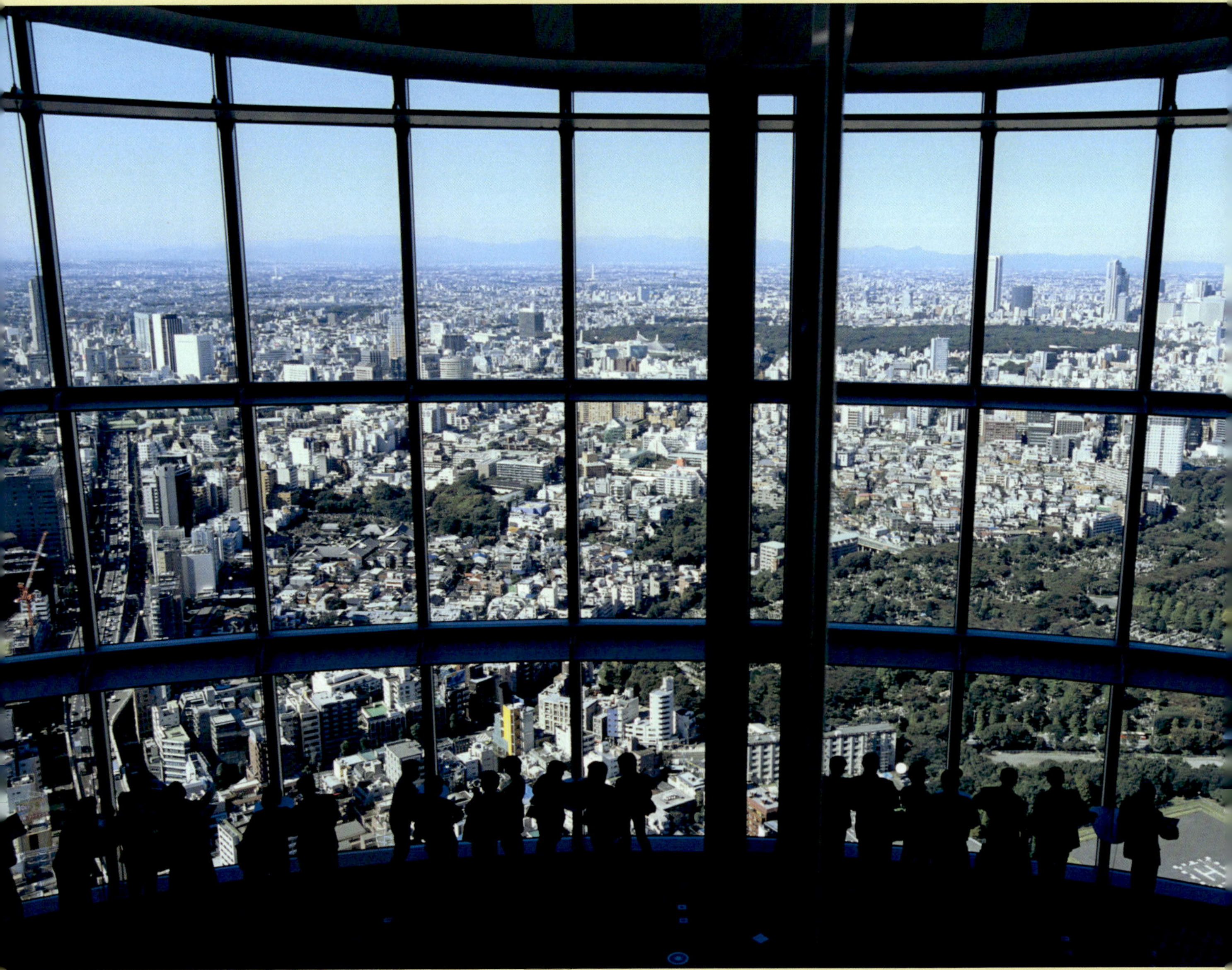

From the observation level of a skyscraper, some of the things people may be able to see include other skyscrapers and buildings; bridges, railway lines and roads; parks, rivers, lakes and oceans, hills and mountains; and of course, people.

Many people on an observation deck enjoy the feeling of being above the city and looking up at the sky.

Many restaurants that operate in skyscrapers make the most of the view. Restaurant workers set up tables near the large windows and people can sit and eat while enjoying the view of the city. Some skyscrapers have a **revolving restaurant** on the top floor, which allows visitors a 360-degree view of the city from their seats.

Sometimes, people celebrate special occasions, such as weddings, in skyscraper restaurants. They include the view of the city in their photographs of the occasion.

Even at street level, the design of a skyscraper is important. Too many skyscrapers built closely together would turn the surrounding roads into cold, dark places.

To avoid this, many skyscrapers are designed with gardens or small parks around their bases, as well as cafes and shops at street level. These features bring open space, colour and light to the area.

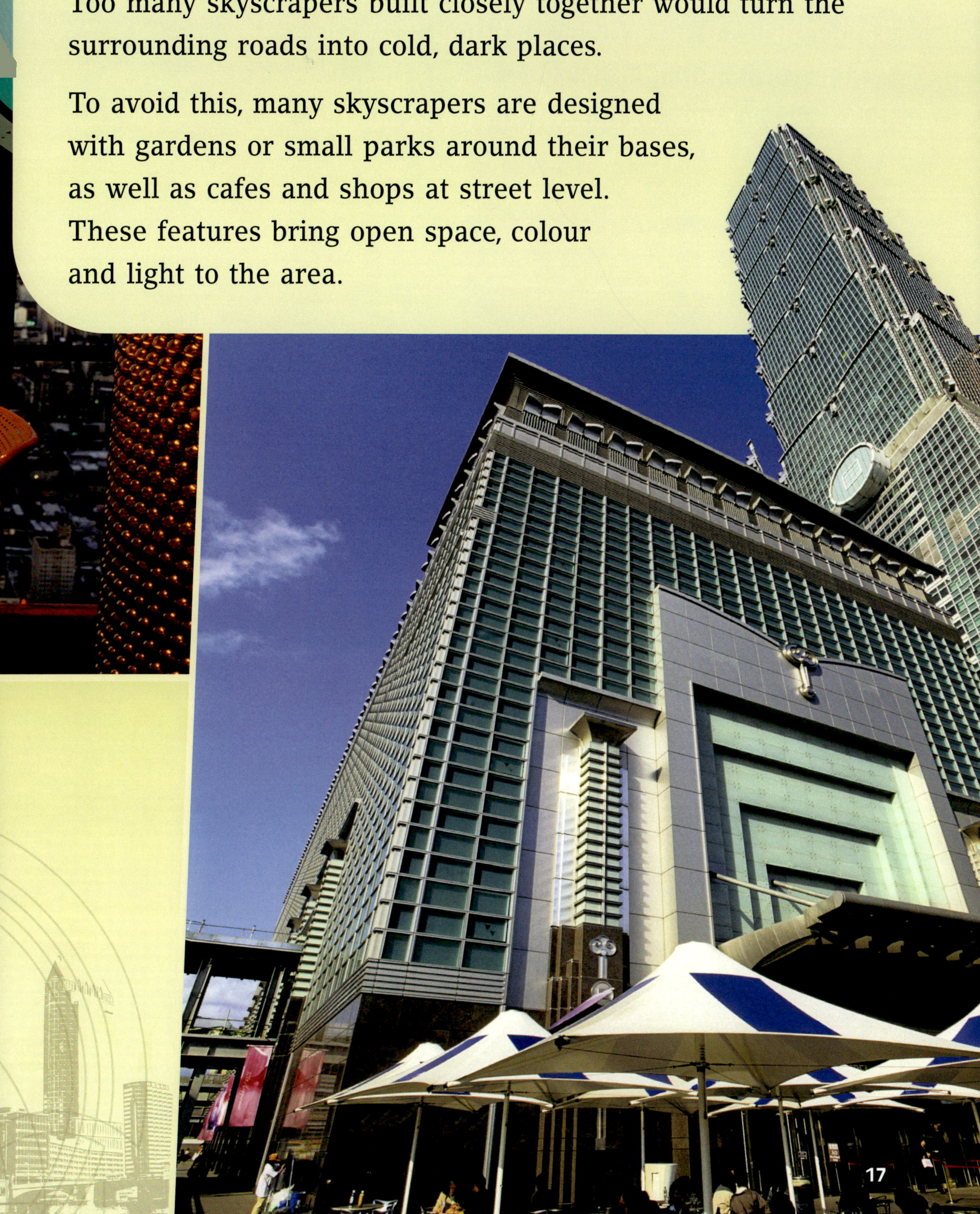

Case Study: Taipei 101

Taipei 101 is a skyscraper in Taipei, Taiwan. When it was finished in 2004, it was the tallest skyscraper in the world at 508 metres.

Taipei 101 Facts

- 508 metres tall
- 101 levels above the ground
- five levels underground
- built on 380 supports that are sunk deep into the ground
- Taipei 101 is named for the 101 levels it has above the ground

the Taipei 101 shopping mall

a bamboo forest

Many modern skyscrapers are designed to reflect the local culture. Taipei 101 is designed to look like a growing bamboo plant, which is a symbol of strength in some Asian cultures.

The number eight is also an important part of the building's design because eight is a lucky number in some Asian cultures. The main body of Taipei 101 has eight parts.

Taipei 101 is built in an area where strong winds and earthquakes occur. The building has been designed to withstand wild weather and earthquakes. People inside the skyscraper may not even feel an earthquake when it happens.

Taipei 101 is also fitted with the latest technology, making it a modern place for living, working and recreation.

Taipei 101 has eight main body parts because eight is a lucky number in some Asian cultures.

New Skyscrapers

New skyscrapers are being designed and built all the time. **Architects** and builders use the latest construction methods and materials to create very tall buildings that are both safe and modern.

Many new skyscrapers have unusual designs to make them look different from other buildings. These impressive designs also help to shape the look of the surrounding cities.

the Turning Torso, Malmö, Sweden

Many people go to see skyscrapers being built and visit them when they are completed.

People watch with interest as taller and taller skyscrapers are built around the world. But no skyscraper stays the world's tallest for long!

Glossary

architects	people who design buildings and oversee their construction
earthquake	the shaking of Earth's surface caused by the movement of underground plates
revolving restaurant	a restaurant that turns 360 degrees
supports	posts for carrying part of the weight of a structure
withstand	to stand or hold out against; to outlast

Index